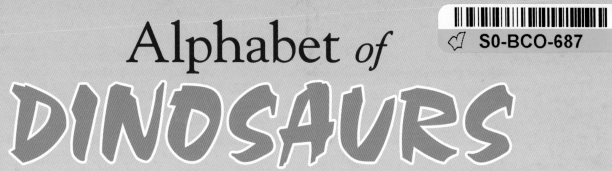

Alphabet *of* DINOSAURS

by Barbie Heit Schwaeber
Illustrated by Thomas Buchs, Karen Carr,
Adrian Chesterman and Trevor Reaveley

SMITHSONIAN INSTITUTION

Book copyright © 2007 Trudy Corporation
and the Smithsonian Institution, Washington, DC 20560.

Published by Soundprints, an imprint of Trudy Corporation, Norwalk, Connecticut.
www.soundprints.com

Illustrations by Thomas Buchs for the cover, poster and the letters E, F, I, K, L, M, R, U, W, X, Y and Z
Karen Carr for the half title page, title page, glossary, poster and the letters D, G, H, J, O, P, S, T and V
Adrian Chesterman for the poster and the letters A and Q
Trevor Reaveley for the poster and the letters B, C and N

Book design: Marcin D. Pilchowski
Editor: Tracee Williams
Production editor: Brian E. Giblin

First Paperback Edition 2008
10 9 8 7 6 5 4 3 2
Printed in China

Acknowledgments:
Our very special thanks to Dr. Michael Brett-Surman and Dr. Matthew T. Carrano of the Smithsonian Institution's
National Museum of Natural History for their curatorial review of this title.
Soundprints would also like to thank Ellen Nanney and Katie Mann at the Smithsonian Institution's Office of Product
Development and Licensing for their help in the creation of this book.

ISBN 978-1-59249-993-9 (pbk.)

The Library of Congress Cataloging-in-Publication Data below applies only to the hardcover edition of this book.

Library of Congress Cataloging-in-Publication Data

Schwaeber, Barbie.

Alphabet of dinosaurs / Barbie Heit Schwaeber ; illustrated by Thomas Buchs ... [et al.].—1st ed.
  p.   cm.
ISBN 978-1-59249-724-9
1. Dinosaurs—Juvenile literature. 2. Alphabet books—Juvenile literature. I. Buchs, Thomas. II. Title.
QE861.5.S345 2007
567.9—dc22

2007029674

Alphabet *of*
DINOSAURS

by Barbie Heit Schwaeber
Illustrated by Thomas Buchs, Karen Carr,
Adrian Chesterman and Trevor Reaveley

Soundprints

A is for Ankylosaurus.
(ang-KIE-lo-SAWR-russ)

This dinosaur used its clubbed tail
to fend off an attack.
If something tried to hurt him
this dinosaur fought back!

Aa

Bb

B is for **Brachiosaurus.**
(BRACK-ee-oh-SAWR-russ)

This dinosaur was one of
the largest of them all.
Its neck was very, very long
but its head was small.

C is for Ceratosaurus.
(sair-RAT-oh-SAWR-russ)

These dinosaurs were carnivores
which means that they ate meat.
They were fierce and roamed the earth
on their strong running feet.

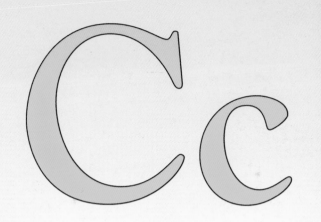

D is for **Dromaeosaurus**.
(DROM-ee-oh-SAWR-russ)

Do you think all dinosaurs were big?
Well, this one was quite small.
It had feathers on its body
and very few scales at all.

Dd

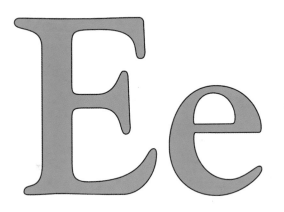

E is for **Edmontosaurus.**
(ed-MON-toe-SAWR-russ)

This dinosaur had three big toes
on its two back feet.
Its hands were shaped like mittens
to walk to food that it could eat.

F is for Fossils.
(FOSS-sils)

Paleontologists study fossils.
It's the only way they know
what dinosaurs might have looked like
millions of years ago.

Ff

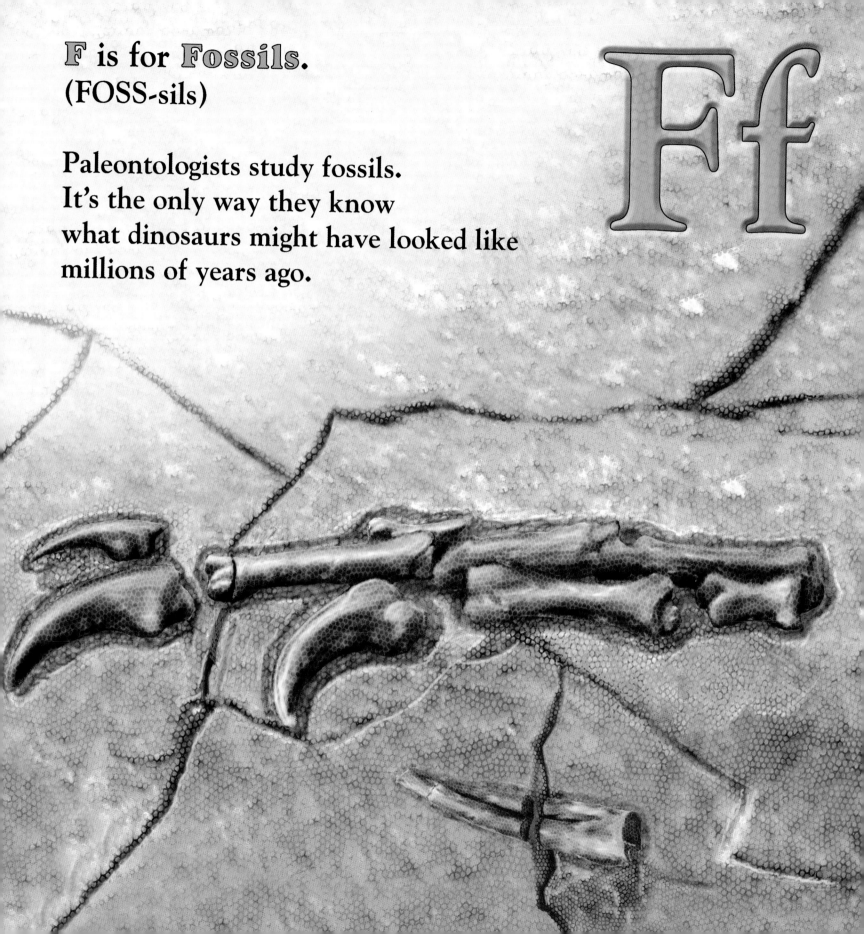

Gg

G is for **Gallimimus.**
(gal-ih-MY-mus)

This dinosaur was bird-like
with a beak and big, round eyes.
It weighed about one thousand pounds
and was quite fast for its size.

H is for Hypsilophodon.
(HIP-sil-LOW-foe-don)

See these plant-eating dinosaurs?
They had teeth inside each cheek.
Those teeth were small and leaf-shaped
and in front they had a beak.

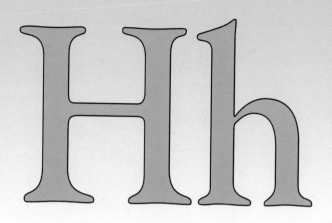

I is for **Iguanodon**.
(ih-GWAHN-oh-don)

An Iguanodon ate only plants.
It had strong teeth and jaws.
You can see it had three toes
and a thumb-spike instead of claws.

Ii

Jj

J is for **Jurassic Period**.
(jur-RAS-sik)

In the Jurassic Period,
birds flew in the air.
There were turtles and evergreen plants,
and dinosaurs everywhere.

K is for **Kentrosaurus.**
(KEN-troh-SAWR-russ)

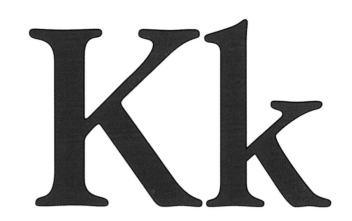

Years ago in Africa
this dinosaur was found.
It held its tail out in the back,
its head close to the ground.

Ll

L is for Lambeosaurus.
(LAM-bee-oh-SAWR-russ)

This dinosaur could weigh six tons.
See the crest upon its head?
It could walk on all four legs
or on its two back legs instead.

M is for **Museum.**
(myoo-ZEE-uhm)

Dinosaurs died long ago but we can all still see them. Let's go on a field trip to the Smithsonian Museum!

N n

N is for Nest.

Look at this big dinosaur.
Her long neck is the best.
She bends down low to check the eggs
in her bowl-like nest.

O is for Oviraptor.
(oh-vee-RAP-tor)

Look closely at this omnivore.
It ate almost everything in sight.
Its legs were long and slender,
and its body swift and light.

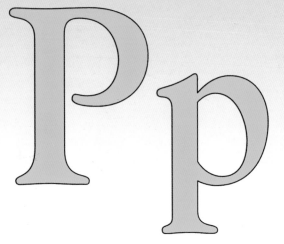

P is for Parasaurolophus.
(par-ah-SAWR-oh-LOH-fus)

Because this dinosaur could splash—
near rivers it was found.
Can you find the big head crest
that helped it make its sound?

Q is for **Quadruped.**
(KWAH-droo-ped)

Did you know that a quadruped
always has four feet?
It walks around on heavy legs
looking for food to eat.

Qq

Rr

R is for **Rhabdodon**.
(RAB-doe-don)

Let's learn about a dinosaur whose name was Rhabdodon. This dinosaur is now extinct which means it is long gone.

S is for Stegosaurus.
(STEG-oh-SAWR-russ)

This dinosaur was very large
but its brain was tiny
(no bigger than a walnut)
and its tail was very spiny.

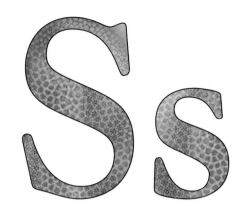

Tt

T is for Tyrannosaurus rex.
(tye-RAN-oh-SAWR-russ rex)

This large meat-eating dinosaur
was able to hunt very well.
Because its eyesight was so clear
as was its sense of smell.

Uu

U is for **Utahraptor**.
(YOO-tah-RAP-tor)

This dinosaur was very fast
when he stalked his prey.
Animals tried to escape him
but they could not get away.

V is for **Velociraptor**.
(vehl-LOSS-ee-RAP-tor)

This dinosaur was found to live
where the climate was hot and dry.
It had sharp claws and it was fierce,
although it only stood three-feet high.

Vv

W is for **Wannanosaurus.**
(wah-NAHN-oh-SAWR-russ)

Why did this dinosaur eat green plants?
Because it was an herbivore.
Nuts and roots and leaves and seeds
were foods for this dinosaur.

X is for **X-ray**.

Would you like to be a scientist
and study dinosaur remains?
With x-ray pictures you can learn
about bones and skulls and brains.

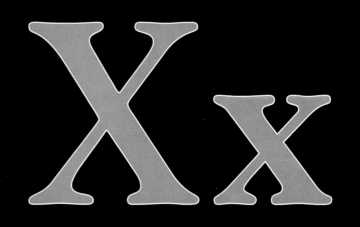

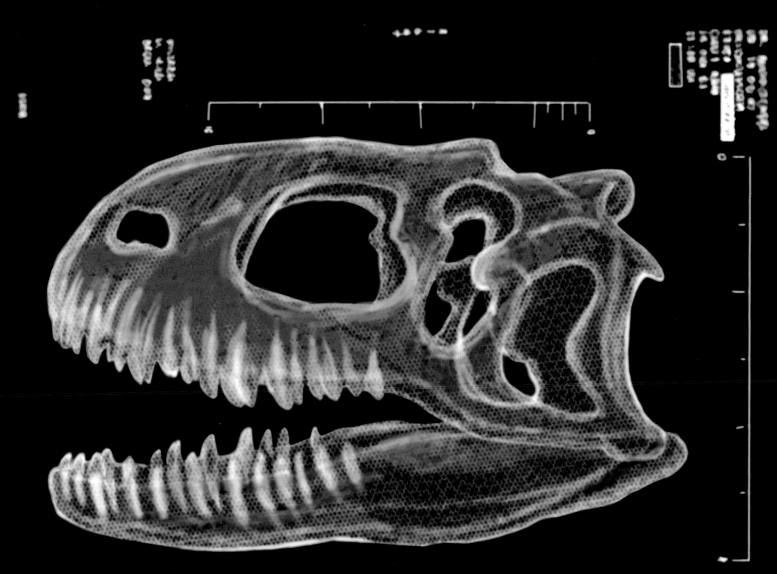

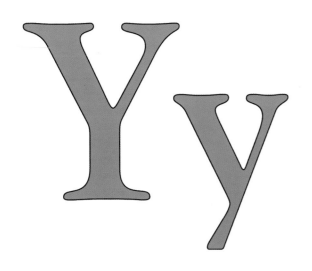

Y is for **Yangchuanosaurus**.
(yang-chew-ANN-oh-SAWR-russ)

Where did this dinosaur come from?
In China its bones have been found.
A theropod walked upright and
that is how it traveled around.

Z is for **Zigongosaurus.**
(zie-GONG-goh-SAWR-russ)

This twenty-ton dinosaur had spoon-shaped teeth.
And here's something you may not know:
This dinosaur's legs were so heavy and thick
and that is why it was so slow.

GLOSSARY

ANKYLOSAURUS: The thick, leathery skin of *Ankylosaurus* was covered with bony plates. These plates help protect *Ankylosaurus* from predators. This dinosaur also had a bony club at the end of its tail that it could swing back and forth to defend itself.

BRACHIOSAURUS: *Brachiosaurus* was one of the tallest and largest dinosaurs ever found. It had a long neck, small head and a short, thick tail. The long neck and stance of this dinosaur almost made it look like a giraffe!

CERATOSAURUS: *Ceratosaurus* was a large, fierce carnivore, or meat eater. Its arms were short and it had hands with sharp claws. It also had two strong feet that helped it to run quickly and a horn on its nose.

DROMAEOSAURUS: *Dromaeosaurus* was a very small, yet fast-moving dinosaur. It was smart and fierce. *Dromaeosaurus* had bird-like eyes that were quite large in comparison to its tiny head.

EDMONTOSAURUS: *Edmontosaurus*, a large duck-billed dinosaur, liked to eat plants with its toothless beak. Its mouth was filled with teeth that the dinosaur used to grind up the plants it ate. It had three toes on its two back feet and it had hands that were shaped liked mittens.

FOSSILS: Fossils are the remains of plants and animals from the geologic past. Fossils are found in layers of rocks. Fossils are important because they help special scientists, called paleontologists, to study the characteristics and behaviors of prehistoric life.

GALLIMIMUS: *Gallimimus* was a fast-running dinosaur with a very long beak. Its neck, tail and legs were also very long. *Gallimimus* was most likely an omnivore, meaning it ate meat, plants, insects and crustaceans—and just about anything else it could get its beak on!

HYPSILOPHODON: *Hypsilophodon* was a small plant-eating dinosaur with a beak made of horn. This fast moving dinosaur lived during the Cretaceous period, about 125 to 120 million years ago.

IGUANODON: *Iguanodon* was a dinosaur that had four fingers plus a thumb-spike on each hand. *Iguanodon* probably used the spikes to defend itself and to get food. *Iguanodon* also had a stiff tail and three-toed feet with hoof-like claws.

JURASSIC PERIOD: The Jurassic Period was a time that took place in the Mesozoic Era, between 199 and 144 million years ago. The first types of birds appeared during this time and many types of dinosaurs roamed the earth.

KENTROSAURUS: *Kentrosaurus* was a plant-eating dinosaur that had plates and spikes on its body. The spikes served as protection from predators. This dinosaur was huge, but probably not too bright—it had a very small brain.

LAMBEOSAURUS: *Lambeosaurus* is one of the largest known duck-billed dinosaurs. It had a huge crest on its head that may have been used to make sounds or help the dinosaur to smell and recognize things.

MUSEUM: A museum is a place for people to visit and learn about different scientific or educational items on display. If you want to learn about dinosaurs, you can go to the Smithsonian Institution's Dinosaur exhibit at the National Museum of Natural History, in Washington, D.C.

NEST: A nest is an area that is made by an animal to house and protect its eggs and its babies. *Apatosaurus* was a type of dinosaur that may have built a nest for her dinosaur eggs. The nests were probably built with sticks, twigs and leaves.

OVIRAPTOR: *Oviraptor* was a small bird-like dinosaur. It had a strong beak and jaws with which it probably ate everything—it was an omnivore. Its legs were long and its hands were large with long, grasping fingers.

PARASAUROLOPHUS: *Parasaurolophus* was an enormous dinosaur with a long, hollow head crest that may have produced sounds. This plant-eating dinosaur could be found near the water. The *Parasaurolophus* walked on its hind legs but hunted on all fours when looking for food.

QUADRUPED: A quadrupedal dinosaur, like *Ankylosaurus*, walked on four feet. Some dinosaurs, like *Ceratosaurus*, were bipedal, meaning they only walked on two feet.

RHABDODON: *Rhabdodon* was a medium-sized plant eating dinosaur that walked on two feet. It had a long tail, a short neck and a beak and its little mouth was filled with large diamond-shaped teeth.

STEGOSAURUS: *Stegosaurus* was a big dinosaur—it weighed about two tons. Its head was also big but its brain was only about the size of a walnut. *Stegosaurus* had large bony plates on its back to help control its body temperature, and possibly for protection.

TYRANNOSAURUS REX: *Tyrannosaurus rex* was the biggest meat-eating dinosaur to live in North America. It weighed up to eight tons! The dinosaur had very good eyesight and a great sense of smell which helped to make it a skillful hunter.

UTAHRAPTOR: This was a large, fierce dinosaur with long finger claws. It was a fast-moving, bird-like dinosaur. *Utahraptor* had very sharp teeth and powerful jaws.

VELOCIRAPTOR: *Velociraptor* was small and light—much smaller than other dinosaurs that existed at the same time. This bird-like dinosaur was probably very smart though. Its brain was large, despite the dinsosaur's small size. This quick little dinosaur was able to change directions rapidly and keep its balance by swinging its tail.

WANNANOSAURUS: *Wannanosaurus* was a small dinosaur—only a few feet long. It was a plant-eating dinosaur that walked on two feet and ran quickly. With its thick, flat-topped skull, it was as strange looking as its name.

X-RAY: An x-ray is a special type of photograph used to study the inside of things, like bones. Scientists use x-rays of fossils to learn about dinosaurs and their biology.

YANGCHUANOSAURUS: This large, powerful dinosaur was a theropod—meaning it was a meat-eater that walked on two large, muscular legs. *Yangchuanosaurus* had large powerful claws.

ZIGONGOSAURUS: This huge dinosaur had a long neck and tail and thick elephant-like legs. It also had spoon-shaped teeth which it used to eat plants. *Zigongosaurus* was named after the area of China in which its fossils were found.